Red Flags

A Handbook for Spotting chi
are co-dependent, enmeshed, abuseu religiously and
emotionally or psychologically –Zac J. Tyler

This book was published thanks to free support and
training from:

EbookPublishingSchool.com

Table of Contents

WOUNDED CHILDREN

HAVE A RAGE, A SENSE OF FAILED JUSTICE

THAT BURNS IN THEIR SOULS.

WHAT DO THEY DO WITH THAT RAGE?

SINCE THEY WOULD NEVER HARM ANOTHER,

THEY TURN THAT RAGE INWARD.

THEY BECOME THE TARGET OF THEIR OWN RAGE.

THEY REPEAT IN THEIR THEIR THOUGHTS

THE SAME HARMFUL WORDS THAT

WERE SPOKEN TO THEM.

THEY MUST LASH OUT,

BUT THE ONLY ONES WEAK ENOUGH

TO ATTACK ARE THEMSELVES.

WOODY HAKEN

I LOVE YOU

I HOPE SOMEDAY YOU SEE THE

BARS THAT WERE NOT LOVE

THEY ARE BARS MADE OF FEAR.

WHEN YOU FINALLY SEE THEM

FOR WHAT THEY ARE

YOU CAN BEGIN TO LEARN TO

LOVE.

WHY I WROTE THIS BOOK

No one is perfect:

Abuse in all forms leaves it's toll, black eyes and broken bones, ruined hearts and damaged minds. No one is perfect. Most people have undesirable personality traits. The amazing thing about humans is that we have a power far greater than the pain and that is the absolute vastness of our minds. Victor Frankl, wrote "Man's Search for Meaning, he was an Austrian neurologist and Freudian psychiatrist who survived the holocaust, but not before losing his mother, father, wife, an unborn child and a brother to the Nazi's and their death camps. Still Dr. Frankl was able to realize something miraculous amidst the pain and stench of death, and that is that no one can take away the freedom found in the deepest recess of our mind.

"Everything can be taken from a man but one thing: the last of the human freedoms—to choose one's attitude in any given set of circumstances, to choose one's own way." – Victor Frankl

WHY YOU SHOULD READ THIS BOOK

As adults we must be the champions for those weaker than ourselves, children are in a vulnerable position in which they must accept whatever situation they find themselves in at home as "normal." Even if normal equals pain and confusion. As adults we can stand guard over these children and provide them with some amount of protection from the world and those who would seek to exploit their inability to fight back. We can put on the armor of wisdom, watch for behaviors that are concerning and take these observations to a higher authority. All to often a child is exposed to abuse only because other adults feel unsure enough to tell an authority when they see a strange behavior or sense that something could be wrong. It is our duty as adults to notice, record and report suspicious activity when it concerns a minor.

Stop the abuse as early as you can, the pain it causes lasts forever.

I am the survivor of narcissistic abuse. It has created many complications in my daily life. Though I do not remember all of the key abuse moments that altered my life forever, the destruction and impact has been devastating to say the least. There are days that are beautiful, full of joy and promise, and then there are days that my family must help me through unspeakable anguish caused by the fall out of years learning that I was not good enough unlovable or trustworthy. I am still fighting the abuse years after the abuser has moved on. I still live in the shadow of the emotional dystopia they hammered into my core being. Even after years of one on one cognitive behavioral therapy and hardcore peeling back of the layers that once defined me as a broken person I feel pain that is almost too much to hold onto.

"TO LEARN WHO RULES OVER YOU, SIMPLY FIND OUT WHO YOU ARE NOT ALLOWED TO CRITICIZE."

- VOLTAIRE

CHAPTER 1. RECOGNIZING PATTERNS IN CHILDREN RAISED BY NARCISSISTIC/ABUSIVE PARENTS

Can you recognize a child who is being abused in a way that does not leave bruises on the skin, no black eyes, no bloodied lip, no falling down the proverbial stairs?

By the end of this small but mighty guidebook, you will be equipped to recognize traits and patterns that children express when they are being forced to share a life with a mentally and emotionally abusive caregiver. This is not a book about how to mitigate these traits once you have recognized them, only how to spot them. Once the signs have been recognized make sure to keep detailed records of instances they occur and then reach out to an authority, a councilor, police officer, social service worker or psychologist to verify your suspicions. For the sake of a child NEVER be afraid to pass on information to the right authority, it could mean the difference between a functional human being and one that is mentally, emotionally and socially crippled for the remainder of their adult lives.

It is harder to spot a child that is suffering from psychological abuse, with so much emphasis placed on recognizing outer wounds as evidence but it is immeasurably important that people are aware that psychological abuse in it's any forms is more prevalent than physical abuse and the effects of the abuse last longer and have deeper impacts than physical abuse.

THE SOCIAL MIRROR

Stephen R Covey the Author of the 7 Habits of Highly effective people explained eloquently the process by which we humans build our core beliefs. He coins the term seeing through a "Social Mirror." This mirror is not an accurate reflection of our self worth, it is simply a collection of what we have been told by others that they feel best describes us. Covey likens the mirror to that of a crazy mirror from a carnival, in which we see ourselves through the distorted projections of others created from their own character flaws and weaknesses. Paul Holinger M.D. writer for Psychology Today explains that the sense of self begins as early the 18th month of life, this is when a child recognize their self in the mirror, begins processing language to later speak and realizes they desire things outside of their parents wants. With this is mind it is critical to understand that if a child is trapped in a home where the caregiver constantly reflects back a negative, unstable or confusing "Social Mirror" for the child that is going to significantly alter the way they develop as a human being, drastically impede that child's ability to see themselves in any other way than broken, incomplete and leave them unable to cope in healthy ways. The damage begins as early as the first year of life and only continues to damage the child deeper and deeper until they reach adulthood, where the problem festers like a deep unknown splinter, damaging different aspects of their lives and leaving them frustrated, fearful, angry and unable to find answers easily. Psychological abuse undermines what children believe about their abilities as a human being, their self worth and how they can manage age appropriate tasks. The mistreatment rearranges or completely destroys positive core beliefs they have about themselves. Dr. Bridget Ross writes a blog entitled "Cognitive Therapy 101" in which she explains that Core Beliefs are the inner dialogue that describes the way we see ourselves, how we view other people and what defines our worldviews and how we feel about our future. We adapt, "truths" about ourselves based on how we think other people view us- this is our social mirror.

ADAPTED TRUTH CHECKLIST

I'm not good enough

I can't get anything right

I'm inferior

I'm unattractive (ugly, fat, etc.)

I'm a failure

I'm abnormal

I do not measure up to others

I don't deserve anything good

I'm a bad person

I'm helpless

When someone is exposed to prolonged experiences where their social mirror tells them that they are defective, the core begins to accept this as a truth. Children and adults that feel they are inherently defective are perfect targets for emotional abusers and Narcissistic personality types that need to keep emotionally damaged people close as a supply to get high. Many times a child will be groomed from birth by an abusive parent to supply a never ending supply and the child will experience the damage as a result of the emotional abuse they are exposed to.

Replacing these core beliefs with uncertainty, fear and a deficit they can never seem to fill especially if they are going to the abuser to gain confidence, love and emotional stability.

Core beliefs are so entrenched in the child that they do not represent what they do, but rather who they are. Though the damage is great, the actual mechanism is elusive, children who are being hurt by people they consider the most precious and trustworthy loved ones may not even realize they are being harmed.

This is a book of checklists and detailed explanations in order to reflag certain behaviors from both child and caregiver to determine if possible abuse is happening. ***This book in not intended to treat or replace medical advice or legal representation.*** If you find that a child or a caregiver has one or more of these signs and behaviors they should then be recorded and reported to appropriate authorities. Never try to convince a child that they are being abused, or intervene alone with the parent. Many times the child will not see what you see and may feel absolute terror of losing the person who is abusing them because they don't understand the situation. If a caregiver/parent or guardian shows a grouping of these tendencies, they are most likely extremely manipulative and crafty or it may be the case that they don't know they are participating knowingly in these behaviors, especially if they are abuse survivors themselves. This book deals primarily with countering the harm caused by "willful" narcissist, people that know they are sick and produce pain from their behaviors but do not care see their behaviors as perfectly acceptable or even powerful and positive traits. In ANY situation, report- do not attempt to solve the issue one on one, these are not healthy individuals and they will require an intervention and a great deal of help if they want to change their behaviors.

Instead make very detailed notes with places, times and experiences that you red flag, then turn to a teacher, school councilor, police officer or social worker to open an investigation. Children are fragile and cannot often see what is happening because they are living in the heart the abuse or neglect.

QUICK FAST MYTH & FACTS

ABOUT MENTAL ABUSE (SOURCE:

HELPGUIDE.ORG)

Psychological Abuse:

Emotional abuse, mental abuse A form of mistreatment in which there is intent to cause mental or emotional pain or injury; PA includes verbal aggression, statements intended to humiliate or infantilize, insults, threats of abandonment or institutionalization; PA results in stress, social withdrawal, long-term or recalcitrant depression, anxiety

McGraw-Hill Concise Dictionary of Modern Medicine. © 2002 by The McGraw-Hill Companies, Inc.

Anything that intentionally hurts the feelings of another person. Since almost everyone in intimate relationships does that at some time or other in the heat of an argument, emotionally abusive behavior must be distinguished from an emotionally abusive relationship, which is more than the sum of emotionally abusive behaviors. In an emotionally abusive relationship, one party systematically controls the other by:

Undermining his or her confidence, worthiness, growth, or trust.

"Gaslighting" - making him/her feel crazy or unstable.

Manipulating him/her with fear or shame.

CHECKLIST FOR RECOGNIZING AN

EMOTIONAL ABUSER

Source: Mateo Sol, Lonewolf Psych spiritual mentors)

☐   **The Engulfing Narcissist** – Parents view their children as   extensions of themselves. They are obsessively involved in a child's life, dictating all norms, have no personal boundaries and do not acknowledge the child as a separate person.

☐   **Ignoring Narcissist**- Parents who have little to no interest in their children. These parents do not bond with their child, see a definite boundary between them and the child and do not show any active interest in the child's life.

☐   **Controlling through co-dependency**- Parents use phrases such as "don't leave me, I can't live with out you." This is to make it impossible for a child to grow independently of the adult and establish his or her own priorities other than catering to the parent.

☐ **Guilt Trips**-Verbalizing how much they have had to sacrifice for the child, making them feel that if they would leave, make friends, tell anyone what was going on – saying that leaving would "break their heart forever." This is to elicit a feeling of helplessness and make the child feel indebted to the parent and to gain complete obedience no matter the personal cost to the child.

☐ **Love that is only available if the child does the right thing**- These parents give and withdraw love easily. If a child fails to do what the parent wants they are punished severely or ignored (the cold shoulder/silent treatment) these children begin to believe that they must "earn" their parents affection and love.

☐ **Boundaries are Non-Existent**- There is no private space for the child, no place to call their own. These parents go through a child's room and their belongings without substantial motive speaking to the child's safety. When something is found the item is used to shame or guilt the child. This can also include sleeping arrangements and private time, such as showering, bathing and dressing after an age where it would be considered unethical and a boundary violation to "help" the child especially of the opposite sex.

☐ **The parents compete with the child for attention**- If the child earns something, the parents take it away. If the child gets something nice, the parents get something nicer to outdo them. This type of parent will see a child's accomplishment as an extension of his or her own accomplishments- "Johnny did well in the track meet because I was an all star runner." "Betty is cute but I was the prettiest girl at the University."

☐ **They are Habitual Liars**-Parents that manipulate, control and take advantage of the child repetitively. The child never quite knows what is real; sometimes they are set up for hidden traps.

☐ **Never Listening to or caring about others feelings**- A child feels that they cannot share their feelings with their parent because they won't be taken seriously, they will be made fun of or they will have an angry outburst or the parent will redirect the topic to "their" feelings. A child's bad day turns into a pity part for mom or dad.

☐ **Constant Insults**-Parents use berating, demeaning statements, and harassment constantly. If a child has insecurity such as being heavy or struggling with school work the parent will exploit that to make them feel even worse during an argument.

☐ **Exercising Explicit Control** – Using the fear of physical or emotional punishment to make a child behave it the way the parent deems appropriate. If the child deviates even slightly from the accepted behavior then the parent comes down with an iron fist. Sometimes the parent emotionally blackmails the child, telling them if they even think about doing something different than what the parent wants, that they will suffer the consequences of a beating.

☐ **Gaslighting** – Making a child unsure of what they remember, or inserting false memories into a conversation. "Remember when you an killed the goldfish? That is why you aren't allowed to have a pet, because you can't be trusted." When the child has NEVER owned or for that matter killed any type of fish. IF the child resists the gas lighting just gets more intense- "Yes you did have a fish, you were just too young to remember. Or you just don't want to remember because you want another fish now." This is a tactic used to control the child through confusion, it deliberately makes them feel crazy and unsure of anything they remember, making them totally dependent on the parent to remember important things for them and instills constant self-doubt.

☐ **The "Golden Child" also** known as the favorite child. These parents pick a favorite child and a scapegoat child. One child is perfect and capable of no wrong; the other is the black sheep of the family, where all the blame lands. To add to the confusion the parent may switch these rolls frequently.

☐ **Inability to Process Criticism-**

These parent general reaction to any type of criticism is to react violently or have emotional outbursts, screaming, physical abuse, kicking the child out or making them call others to apologize for their terrible behaviors, in order to shame them and make them submissive.

☐ **Projecting their Bad behaviors onto the child**-A parent that reacts to a child's bad day or request by screaming at them or hitting them, then tells them to go tot their room until they can calm down and not scream or be physical.

☐ **Non Empathetic**- They don't care about the child's feelings, they cannot sympathize or care because they only are invested in their own feelings.

☐ **Infallibly Correct and Never Wrong**- When they make a mistake or treat someone poorly and are called on it to correct it they refuse to own up and admit the fault. This parent will deny all accusations and spin the blame to project on someone else.

If you answered yes to more than just a couple of these you maybe looking at a very destructive and manipulative parent/caregiver and a child in need of serious intervention, support and counseling.

CHECKLIST FOR RECOGNIZING AN EMOTIONALLY ABUSED CHILD

Children experience a myriad of emotional, mental and physical changes, which makes pinpointing emotional abuse very hard. There are guidelines that experts have established that may be red flags during different developmental stages. (Source: nspcc.org.uk)

YOUNGER CHILD

☐ Infants and children young enough to attend preschool may exhibit **overly affectionate behaviors towards complete strangers** or people that they have not known very long.

☐ They may **lack self-confidence, seem guarded and anxious.**

☐ They may seem **to not have a connection with their guardian or parent** when being dropped off or picked up from the facility.

☐ They may **express their frustration by lashing out** at teachers, peers and animals, being aggressive or nasty or extreme towards these groups. A five-year-old female expressed anger and violent ideations during a playground encounter when she pushed another child from the swing set and physically assaulted her for unknown reasons. When asked why she attacked the other child she said simple "It feels good to hurt other people, I like it." She was in the middle of a nasty divorce that includes two narcissistic personality type parents that were physically and emotionally volatile towards one another. She witnessed her father push her mother down a flight of stairs and was told she was the reason that the marriage was ending. Pretty heavy accusation for five years old.

Older children may

Use language that is far beyond their comprehension or know about topics that are not age appropriate. Big words aren't always a red flag, however adult concepts may be a warning since this indicates that a child I s parroting an abusive adult and is being directed and cued to say and think only what the adult wants them too. This can also be seen as bizarre thinking- putting things together that do not make sense such as "I cant go to that chaperoned organized event because they will be staying in a hotel/camp and that isn't safe" or "I can't talk to a councilor because I only trust my family."

Struggle to control strong emotions and have extreme outbursts- A 12 year old boy from a severally enmeshed cultic and narcissistic home showed explosive aggressive episodes in which he felt like he could not stop and was on a violent loop no matter how much anger he released. He would also have frequent ideations of violence and fighting in which he vanquished the "bully." This may be a result of the child not feeling that he has any control in his situation and using daydreams to insert a scenario where he is strong self-reliant and can protect himself in his mental space.

☐ **Seem isolated from other people**- because a very common tactic for emotional abusers is to isolate and use this isolation to deploy thought control, where the child has no other well of knowledge to draw from so they cannot compare what is normal against what is happening even if they feel like something is wrong.

☐ **Lack social skills or have few, if any friends**- this can be the direct result of in-appropriate social cueing, cultic family structure and parental/ guardian induced isolation and fear mongering about the outside world. It can also be a flag for certain types of high functioning autism, but this needs to be tested and verified by a professional. Children on the spectrum need support catered to their specific needs. If the child in question has exhibited more than a few of these characteristics high functioning autism may not be the issue.

Key Words

Some key words that pop up when dealing with emotionally traumatized and abused children:

Obsessive Behaviors- Withdrawn- Hates School- Aggressive-Problems Sleeping-Wets the Bed- Anxious- Clingy- Unsure what they are "allowed" to talk about with another adult-Takes Risks-Nightmares-Drugs and Alcohol- Suicidal Ideations-Soils Clothes- Depressed-Behaves Erratically-Mood Shifts Quickly-Eating Disorders.

These signs don't necessarily mean that a child is being emotionally abused, look for behaviors that seem out of character for the child, realize that teenagers have many challenging behaviors as they learn to cope with the changes in their body, mind and social world.

Symptoms may take a long time to show, especially if the child is trying to protect their abuser, they may purposely attempt to hide behaviors that might give the hurt away to outsiders. Often these children do not have a clear sense of where their feelings begin and their abusive parent/ guardians feelings end, effectively the caregivers strong and over powering emotions often overlay directly on top of the child's smothering the child's ability to feel for themselves and separate their needs, emotions and feelings from the abusers. This is why an astute or intelligent child may try to cover their tracks, understanding that many of their parents/ guardians behaviors are not acceptable they still want to protect them in order to also protect themselves. In this case they are not separate people, they are one in the same, what hurts the abuser hurts the child.

These are the signs, but now we need to discuss what the implications and outcomes are for children suffering under these abusive parent types.

THE EFFECTS OF

PSYCHOLOGICAL/ EMOTIONAL

ABUSE

Emotional abuse is more harmful than physical abuse for many reasons: Physical abuse often occurs in cyclical patterns

1. Violent Outburst

2. Honeymoon Period of Remorse

3. Attentions and Affection

4. Generosity/ Not Genuine Affection

Eventually many victims of domestic physical abuse will reach the honeymoon or later stages and realize that the abuse is going to happen again and again and they find a way to leave the situation. The effects of psychological and emotional abuse are more destructive because there is no clear cycle, no downtime between incidents it is just a constant barrage of day to day incidents that undermine everything positive and strong about the victim. Emotional abuse is more personal, it attacks who you are as a person, it attacks who you are spiritually, and it makes love, which should be a shelter and a rock, unstable, poisonous and hurtful.

SHORT TERM EFFECTS OF PSYCHOLOGICAL/ EMOTIONAL ABUSE

Hopeless, Helplessness, Walking on Eggshells, Unable to discuss certain topics with others.

Passivity to the Abuse, Self Doubt, Low Self Esteem and Low Self Confidence.

Eye Contact Avoidance.

Explosive Emotions, Self-Harm.

Anxiety, Guilt, Shame.

Psychological and Emotional Abuse/Acute

Short Term Effects of Psychological Abuse radiate out from the abuse creating Guilt, Shame and Anxiety, which can then manifests as Explosive Emotional states. If you pull a rubber band back far enough eventually it will snap back with the same amount of force and energy it was pulled with often resulting in mentally and emotionally catastrophic mini events for the abused. Making them seem to be the unstable person in the relationship and not the abuse. Many times abusers will capitalize on this "snap back" and use it to "prove" to outside observers that the child is not stable, is "bad" or has an undiagnosed learning disability. This effectively removes any blame or speculation from the abuser and places the full weight on the fragile child who is simply trying to survive the situation. Be aware when dealing with a potentially abused child that their "bad" behaviors may simply be the aftershocks of having their feelings and needs repressed and denied repeatedly.

The longer the child lives with mental or emotional abuse the more they begin to normalize the behaviors of the caregiver as a coping strategy. A child that has experienced prolonged abuse may become angry or resistant when shown evidence that their caregiver is harming them; this is because the caregiver is the sole provider of all things that the child knows to be true and safe.

"ROOM SYNDROME"

The mentally abused child is stuck in a parallel reality that I coined "Room Syndrome" ™ this is not a psychiatric term, you will not find it in the DSM V (Diagnostic and Statistical Manual of Mental Disorders) it is my own interpretation of how the abuse child views their life inside of the care of the abuser.

As a survivor of several types of abusive behavior I can accurately describe my world as a child and as an abused adult as that of being mentally stuck in a room and not knowing that there was anything on the other side of the walls. I had an idea that things weren't normal, being bright and curious and I even lashed out in anger expressing that I was smart enough to know that something wasn't right but still my family was my first contact with culture and how society worked. As much as I "felt" things were off, I had a hard time expressing that because- for all of the evidence my feelings gave me; the family mirror told me that it was normal inside of our four walls. Wrestling with that inability to tell what is normal from abnormal harmed me more times than I can recall as I entered into adulthood, it effects everything from peer relationships, romantic interests to ability to find suitable or sustainable employment.

Recently a movie that was released that depicted a child born to a woman who had been kidnapped and placed inside a locked room, the boy grew up knowing nothing of the outside world, in effect all that the child knew to be real was inside of the "room." All things the child read about or heard about that were not part of room were thought of as fantasy.

The woman participated in these delusions to protect her child because she saw no way out of the room until a later time. At that time she came up with a plan and needed her child's help to carry it out, the problem was, the child was not prepared to leave "room" because it was his universe not a simple room, in his mind there was nothing outside of the four walls but the cold vacuum of outer space and that terrified him deeply. The mother wanting to prepare him tried to explain that there was an enormous beautiful place with family that loved him, animals, vehicles, plants and wide open spaces outside of the room. He struggled because these were not the concrete experiences he knew, only abstract possibilities and initially the child unsurprisingly chose the "devil he knew over the one he didn't" because even though the room was a small, dangerous place that was unsuitable for the child, he knew he could find security on some aspects of it. He would rather stay with the predictable heartbreak and collect the scraps of sanctuary available to him than venture out and save himself, his mother and potentially gain an entire universe of better possibilities.

The child in room was locked in a physical room; the abused child is locked inside a mental room. I won't provide a spoiler for the film, but the parallels drawn are chillingly accurate for a child who is immersed in psychological or emotional abuse at home. With this in mind understand that consulting a professional councilor or psychologist who has a specialty in understanding this type of abuse is paramount in helping the childfree him or herself and then begins to heal. This isn't something that can be easily accomplished just by removing the child physically, even out of the physical radius of the abuser the harm caused by their experiences will stick into the child's emotional health like glass shards, working it's way in deeper and deeper until it causes long-term issues far into their adult life. Emotional abuse is a lingering poison that must be treated in the long term to mitigate its effects. In order for a child to leave their mental room they will need a very well trained guide that can read between the lines and see when a child is being abused no matter how smooth or convincing the abuser may seem.

LONG-TERM EFFECTS OF PSYCHOLOGICAL/EMOTIONAL ABUSE

Long-term issues that children face after sustaining abuse for a long period of time are varied. They may develop risk-taking behaviors such as

Stealing

Bullying

Running Away.

They may begin to exhibit mental health problems, eating disorders and self-harming. Abuse is linked to stunting of emotional development, red flags for children who may be experiencing psychological abuse include:

The inability to express a full range of emotions appropriately.

Issues controlling their emotions.

Exhibiting angry emotional outbursts.

Children who have love and attention withheld from them have great difficulty later developing and maintaining healthy relationships with other people later in life.

The rest of the chapters will involve diving deeper into specific modes of emotional abuse.

"NOT ALL SCARS SHOW, NOT ALL WOUNDS HEAL

SOMETIMES YOU CAN'T ALWAYS SEE,

THE PAIN THAT SOMEONE FEELS."

CHAPTER 2. WHEN THE
CAREGIVER IS A NARCISSIST

It will be interesting to anyone who has met a narcissist to hear that recent research suggests that adults that show these traits most likely had formed their damaging personality traits completely by the age of seven! What is a narcissist? There are varying levels of narcissistic traits people can express and not be a true Narcissist. Most of us have little personality quirks that are inherently more selfish than we like, the differences between feeling selfish once in a while and having this personality disorder is that you are aware of your issues and most likely annoyed by them, feel some level of guilt for the pain or frustration they cause others and may even be consciously working towards eliminating socially harmful behaviors. The Narcissist is COMPLETELY aware that their behaviors are cruel and further more they do not only not care that they are destroying other people with their behaviors they see these traits as positives and power indicators. They are a black hole that is constantly searching for energy sources, your emotions, the higher the better are the perfect food source for this type of personality. They will pull you up and then slam you down to get the most energy out of your emotional stores as they can. So how do you recognize a parent or guardian who's negative personality traits are so impactful that they could be described as abuse? Do you recognize any of these traits in the parent you feel may be abusing a child?

Is the Parent/Guardian in question a Narcissist or have Narcissistic Qualities?

Check List

The parent/guardian "lives" through their child- *Narcissistic caregivers set goals that have no benefit for the child, they only wish to fulfill their selfish wants and needs. The child is not allowed to have their own thoughts and wishes, to think differently than the caregiver is to attack their ego. The child is not afforded individuality and must be an extension of the parent/caregiver.*

They Practice Marginalization

Narcissistic parent sees their child's potential, promise or success as a direct challenge to their own self-esteem. They counter any personal achievement by invalidating them immediately. These caregivers utilize nit picking, unreasonable judgment, impossible and unfavorable comparisons to other people/siblings, ignoring when the child does something good and rejects their success and their accomplishments as valid enough to be praised.

They are grandiose and believe they are Superior to everyone else. *Narcissistic people have a falsely inflated self-image and are conceited about* who they are and what they do. In the eyes of the narcissist a child is not a human being, they are simply a tool or object to be used for gratification and personal gain. This can be seen in action as the narcissistic car giver tries to forge a "we are separate/better than they are" superiority complex within the child. This bond is exclusively based on superficial, egotistical, material or religious trappings and comes at the expense of the child's social needs and humanitarian needs.

They Maintain a Superficial Image. *Regardless of what Intel you have gathered on the parent/guardian concerning disturbing or damaging behaviors from either the child reporting these behaviors or seeing the fallout from them the caregiver will carefully construct a bomb proof outer shell for public view. They will decorate this shell with superior dispositions, material wealth, strong/ attractive physical appearance, and religious fervor, using social media to post an inordinate amount of pictures showing how happy everyone is, share inspirational messages that don't match their actual motives or personal actions, they collect powerful contacts and friends in high places, acquiring trophy mates and raising seemingly model children who also have a strong front. These people make sure that they world outside of the home is convinced that their life is amazing, secure and normal by networking on social media and keeping up a daily front to convince others.*

Since the deception is all about rubbing their own egos they can post for hours at a time and never get sick of the game. This carefully constructed lie is especially damaging to the child, who may feel confused that their personal experiences don't match the outside front that the caregiver is putting up. They may feel it is useless to tell anyone about the abuse since they wouldn't be believed any way or their caregiver would go unpunished because others respect or fear their parent/guardian too much.

They are MANIPULATIVE

They never approach situations or relationships without a motive; if they are talking to you they are trying to figure out how they can get you to do something for them. To keep abusing the child they may employ subtle or heavy alienation with other family members and society in greater context. This can include limiting their contact with important family members, mom, dad, and grandparents and outside sources of support such as teachers, police officers and councilors. If they are unable to physically isolate the child they can teach them ideas such as – other people aren't safe! Only family is safe, if they aren't "me" "our immediate family" "blood relatives" they don't care enough about you to help you and you can't trust them. Or the Narcissistic parent/guardian will employ fear to make sure the child stays put and provides a constant supply of emotional fuel. "If you tell anyone about what we do in our home, they will take you away and put you in foster care, or put me in jail! Then I won't love you anymore" or "If they took you away my heart would be so broken, I'd never recover." To keep other people out of their business the narcissistic parent may give "just enough" time with the child to other people, but not enough time to really understand what is happening in their home or get them help. When the child is with another person they may call constantly, text or demand that a certain time be allocated just for them to speak with the child. Then they "Love Bomb" the child by assuring them that they miss them, they feel empty without them, they won't be happy until they come back and that they will be coming back to where it is safe and they are loved the most soon.

Inflexibility *Narcissistic/ Emotionally Abusive parents/guardians can be highly ridged when they set out expectations for their children. They often micromanage down to the last minor detail and become highly volatile/irrational when there is even slight deviation from their expectations. This inflexibility springs from the parents desire to control the child, when the child refuses to be controlled as if they were a puppet this triggers the caregivers insecurity and they do whatever is necessary to gain back total control. This type of parental control is devastating and can manifest in several ways, the children may **FIGHT** back and try to stand up for themselves. Second the child may **FREEZE** and begin to adopt a fake persona to present around the parent* *to ward off unwanted reactions, in this they may begin to exhibit narcissistic qualities themselves. Third being difficult for a child but something that many adults of narcissistic parents do is to resort to* **FLIGHT** *or* **NO CONTACT.**

Dependency/Co-Dependency *Narcissistic or emotionally abuse parents often start grooming their dependents to take care of them for the rest of their lives. This is not your normal positive parent relationship in which out of love the child grows up and wants to care for the aging parent/guardian. This is forced care, by guilt, manipulation, fear and feeling an unhealthy sense of duty to continue caring for a person that is extremely toxic and harmful to their own needs and lives. The parent/guardian makes unreasonable requests and manipulates the child to support them in unnecessary and inappropriate ways – such as taking over the adult role because the parent is immature, raising siblings, being emotionally dependent on the child or demanding financial assistance because the parent won't fulfill their own obligations. Caring for ones family is an admirable trait, this level of care however is anything by admirable, it is sick, needy and asks that a child or adult child make unreasonable sacrifices with no regard for their own needs and priorities.*

Jealousy & Possessiveness *The emotionally abusive parent expect that the child will never leave their side* *or influence, providing them with an unlimited supply of emotional and ego fulfillment. When the child attempts to grow in maturity or independence outside of that influence the guardian/ parent will feel hostile towards new friends, love interests and powerful influencers such as potentially threatening safety nets - tea*chers, police, councilors etc. They *will feel hostile because these people will be seen as interlopers that are ruining the control dynamic over their emotional food source that they have been working so hard to perfect. The ultimate question they will pose when going through excessively unhealthy separation anxiety due to a child making new friends, trusting new people or creating their own priorities is "How can you do this to ME?"*

Neglect *this is a situation that sends up obvious red flags and is easy to spot. The emotionally abusive parent/guardian that chooses to neglect the child altogether to attend to their own self absorbing activities which they find more exciting and fulfilling than childrearing. This provides the narcissist their excessive self-importance, stimulation and validation – and typical examples are addictions, career obsession, social life, hobbies and personal adventures. Others can misinterpret this as a string of selfish actions but it is far beyond simple selfishness, it becomes emotional and physical neglect and hurts a child deeply to realize they play second*

best to something so trivial as a job, a substance or
an activity.

A DEEPER LOOK INTO WHAT NPD

PARENTING DOES TO A CHILD

The child of a Parent/Guardian with NPD
(Narcissistic Personality Disorder) will display
similar signs as any child who is experiencing
emotional abuse. Seen in the charts in Chapter one.
A deeper explanation of the impact this type of
abuse has on a child is that society in general allows
for this type of abuse to continue unnoticed because
the abuse is so devious and so subtle that it does not
draw attention until the child does something
drastic by acting out. Then it is the child who is
punished or blamed for their negative and anti-
social behavior.

The children of these parents/ guardians are truly
victims the NPD parent is sly, they are devious and if
they know what they are doing, they may even enjoy
the suffering they cause. The success of the NPD
parent/guardian lies in the fact that they are so
subtle that no one outside of the family unit would
ever expect anything is wrong let alone that there is
severe emotional abuse and mental trauma being
experienced by a helpless child. This allows the

child to go unnoticed and untreated, completely under the radar of any authority that could help them.

The key to recognizing the covert abuse is recognizing the imbalance.

Something is obvious.sy wrong with the child. They display major aspects of emotional abuse.

Parent seems "too perfect" they refuse to let anyone really assess the situation or try to figure out what is causing the behaviors. They may have a ready excuse such as a "disorder" they refuse to get a diagnoses for.

The overriding behavioral sign to seeing past the facade of an emotionally abusive parent/guardian is to realize that they have a total lack of concern for the actual child. Even these people with there carefully designed games are not perfect, if the heat is turned up on them they may show weakness and their mistakes will spotlight their NPD.

A key to interacting with these types of individuals (and exposing them for what they are) is to refrain from communicating with them in transient ways- such as a passing conversation that they could later use manipulative tactics such as *__gaslighting__ (later in the book) or twisting your words. Instead use a more permanent medium to interact- such as texting or email, where you can store each conversation, then later access it if it is necessary to show others the inappropriate or unstable behaviors you have been experiencing. NPD and other types of emotionally abusive people often do not see beyond their own game and do not recognize that they make themselves vulnerable by writing there tangents and odd quips on social media, in email or in text messages that can be saved, printed and shared later. These modes of conversation also have a convenient time stamp, which leads to further credibility on your part.

DOCUMENT~ DOCUMENT~ DOCUMENT! If you think that an emotionally manipulative adult may be abusing a child, keep records! Anytime something happens write it down, screen shot, print it out it or get audio confirmation if possible. This is valuable evidence that could later save that child from further harm.

The truth is spotting one of these abusers is hard, because there are varying degrees of NPD. One commonality is no matter where on the spectrum these parents land- they have NO regard for their child's need for individuality, ambition, or emotional health. The NPD person will be extremely charismatic and charming, they use this trait to "groom" others as supply for their exhaustive emotional void, they may be people you thought you could trust, such as your pastor, or a teacher that seems popular with the kids, a successful business man who exudes confidence and material success or a woman that seems to like taking in little chicks under her wing and seems almost "too protective "for the level of actual intimacy you share.

These people aren't simply abusive to their children they are also capable of abusing you or anyone else if they get lucky enough to groom you and hook you up to them as a supply. Look for these behaviors in possible NPD people.

CLASSIC NPD CHARACTERISTICS

Actions:

Love Bombs you

Feigns interest in things you like

Pays inordinate amounts of attention to you

Obsessively aware of what makes you happy

Lavish you with gifts to get you to commit to a relationship at an inappropriately early time for serious commitment

Charming, Charismatic, leave you feeling warm and safe before you know them.

Will change from being loving, wonderful, attentive to raging, unfeeling and cruel.

The effects of being parented by someone with Narcissistic Personality Disorder are far reaching and continue to harm even into adulthood. Often children then turn into adults that have a host of self-defeating issues that plague their ability to interact normally and carry on with healthy relationships. Once you have noted a few signs that a child may be experiencing this type of abuse it is extremely important to move quickly and involve professionals to assess the situation. If you are wrong, you can only be faulted for being overly cautious if you are right you will be able to possibly mitigate a host of later issues that may ruin an adult child of NPD's life.

(As an adult you can recognize these issues in yourself, others or in children that are reaching dating age)

LONG-LASTING EFFECTS OF NPD

Insecure Attachments

*While everyone has the need to be close to others and exhibit a rational dose of dependency on those they feel are trust worthy, the sufferer of NPD parenting has a hard time understanding what is safe or not, and when it is appropriate to depend on people for certain emotional needs. Some abused people will **AVOID** any kind of commitment, romantic or childbearing. The term for those type of reaction is called "**Avoidant Attachment**" it is safer for them to never depend on any one ever again than risk being hurt. It is also safer for them to assume that they will be that type of parent and rationalize that it would be cruel to bring a child into the world to let it go through what they did. The abuse was so great that they doubt their own ability to realize if they are producing the same harmful behaviors with possible children and so they choose to bypass the possibility completely. These tactics allow the abused person to feel that they can keep control of the situation, however the fears that they felt as a child are still deeply embedded in their psyche. Others will choose to engage in risky attachments and become overly dependent very quickly. The term for this type of coping is "**Anxious Attachment**" and it can lead to very unsafe social and romantic obsessions later in life. The young person with this disorder may throw themself at long lines of unworthy, uncaring, unstable partners, this causes them great emotional distress* *because the Anxious person only wants to be loved and reassured, but the amount of reassurance borders or crosses over into obsessive. This eventually drives away healthier suitors and is a beacon for predatory types of lovers and "friends."*

Chronic Self-Blaming

People that grew up with NPD parents learn very fast that if they tried to change certain behaviors that maybe they could mitigate the fallout – it was not a science and often failed but when it worked it was a welcomed relief. The thinking behind trying to this as a child was that they were taught to believe that the emotional abuse was somehow their fault. They came to think of themselves as the problem, if maybe I worked harder, if I made more money, If I cleaned the house better, If I got better grades, then the yelling, anger, criticizing will stop. They carry this belief into adulthood and into relationships and social situations, which aren't usually very stable or fulfilling for them.

Echoing Emotions

Children who grow up in narcissistic homes are often barraged and attacked by their parent/caregivers explosive emotional outbursts, these episodes likely come on right as the child tries to express their own deep emotion or a need. The child expresses fear; the parent is completely dismissive and belittles the importance of the feelings. The child cries about something and the parent explodes with white-hot anger, the child expresses a need to have some independence and the parent collapses sobbing giant tears of fear. The problem for the child is that they grow up never quiet expressing their own emotion; their voice is lost in the echo of their parent emoting back at them forcefully.

Absolute Independence *Another form of avoidant attachment, the children grow up to completely distrust others and will not enter into an emotional relationship, not even a friendship for fear they will be hurt again.*

Compulsive Caregiver *Children who are very sensitive and empathetic may see this as a strength, others may even tell them it is a asset to give everything emotional reserve they have into caring for other people. These grown children will act extremely selfless; they only enjoy life and warmth through sensing they are creating it in other people. They cannot generate their own feelings of happiness and security. This lifestyle is not emotionally healthy and leaves the person at risk if they find someone that they cannot satisfy, thereby not producing "good" feelings for them to recharge under.*

Obsessive Parent Orientated Child *Also sensitive and empathetic these children grow up to take care of their aging narcissistic parents. They focus all of their energy into fulfilling every last wish that the already* extremely needy and selfish parent has. These people are extremely aware of neediness as a negative trait, having experienced the burden of it as a child. However they will worry endlessly that **they** are too needy or too selfish and they hate the thought of burdening others with their own issues.

Repeating the Narcissism *Since the child was not able to find a way to mitigate the pain that the parent doled out during their narcissistic behaviors they then adopt the behavior as their own. If you are tough enough to block everyone out and be the best, toughest, most important, meanest, scariest, loudest or perfect person in the room, no one can hurt you!*

PTSD *This is recognizable by the anxiety, intrusive memories of abuse, inability to visualize a future and feeling generally numb emotionally.*

Self Harm *Cutting is only one form of self-harm, abused people may cut, hit themselves, choke themselves, pull their hair out, punch themselves and scream hateful things at themselves. Eventually they may commit suicide as well.*

CHAPTER 3. SELF HARM

"I HURT MYSELF TODAY

TO SEE IF I STILL FEEL

I FOCUS ON THE PAIN

THE ONLY THING THAT'S REAL"

-TRENT REZNOR NIN

I would like to take a moment to discuss self-harm in particular. Self-harm is one of those extremely physical and easy to spot characteristics of a child or adult that has been or is being emotionally abused. It is important not to assume the self- harmer is simply looking for attention or shock value, self harm is not an action for anyone but the abused. In many cases when a person who has been abused reaches the stage of grief, PTSD or frustration that they engage in self harm they will take themselves away from other people- children are less likely to take themselves into another location such as locking themselves in the bathroom. They self injure right in the moment because the feelings are so strong they cannot stop the compulsion to do so. People who self harm are aware it is not a "normal" behavior, they are often embarrassed by the compulsion, and being judged is a very real fear for these people. Mark Dombeck, Ph.D. of MentalHealth.net explains why people self-harm.

6 Reasons People Self Harm

1.   **To regain control**, alter the focus of their attention, to slow down their minds when experiencing pressing, unavoidable and overwhelming feelings or thoughts. Self-harm interrupts intrusive and uncontrollable thoughts that people are having. By thought stopping for even a second, the person is able to hijack a sense of subjective control and shift their emotions and focus away from the emotional chaos they are feeling.

People sometimes harm themselves because by doing so, they are able to gain a subjective sense of control over **chaotic internal emotions** and thoughts. Seizing this control involves shifting the focus of their attention away from something more troubling towards something less troubling. This is because cutting, strangulation, burning and hitting ones self is a very compelling and strong sensation that the brain cannot ignore.

2.   Release tension associated with strong emotions or overwhelming thoughts. Another aspect of regaining some control, self harm releases the extreme amount of emotional pressure that is building and the chaos being created by the accompanying anxiety attack or melt down that is most likely taking place. When I am experiencing this type of meltdown I begin to loop rapidly, often saying the same word in a sentence over and over again, not stuttering but looping a specific word because my brain is stuck. I will say the word four or five times before I can complete the thought. At this point I am physically vibrating or shaking with emotional frustration, my entire body may be bouncing, rocking or shuddering. Sometimes I go to my knees and hug them in attempt to stop the physical reaction or I take a shower to alter my actual body temperature in hopes that if my core temperature rises I will begin to feel calmer. This may release the tension; if it does not then self-harm is usually not far away. The tension caused by an extreme anxiety melt down is so painful that it is not unrealistic to assume that a relatively resourceful person will seek ways to relieve it. A child may rock, or vibrate, stutter or say how bad or stupid they are over and over and over again, they may also kick doors, throw objects, punch walls and hot their head. If the behavior is compulsive and repetitive, you may be seeing a psychotic/ emotional meltdown in progress. DO NOT Ignore a hysterical child that purposefully injures themselves!! Listen to hear if they are repeating hateful things to themselves- this is HUGE sign that something that is TOO BIG for them to process is happening in their lives.

3.   **To Return From Numbness**

People with significant trauma can cope by disassociating. A disassociation episode can make the person feel separate from their own feelings, who they are, they may not even recognize themselves. The person compartmentalizes different aspects of himself or herself, thereby locking away the most harmful from the person so that they do not have to feel these overwhelming traumas over and over again. At times the person may not even remember the events that hurt them. The parts that are hidden away from the person are replaced by numbness, and it is even more terrifying than feeling pain. Causing self injury can bring a person back from that numbness, it can "wake up" the memories, the reality and the emotional function if only for a moment.

4.   Express themselves or communicate and/or document strong emotions they are feeling and cannot otherwise articulate.

5.   Punish themselves. When a child has been raised in an environment where they experience constant aggression and anger they will feel that they "deserve" to be punished when they are sad or have upset their caregiver. This is what they have been taught, so this is where they go when they are overwhelmed with negative emotion.

6.   **Experience a temporary but intense feeling of euphoria** that occurs in the immediate aftermath of self-harm.

SELF HARM CHECKLIST

Many times children with major depression will display disruptive behaviors such as:

- ☐ Scratching themselves
- ☐ Biting themselves
- ☐ Banging head against the wall
- ☐ Hitting them selves in the head, legs and other parts of self
- ☐ Punch the wall or kick the wall in order to hurt themselves

Children do this because it quickly reduces tension in the mind and body caused by feelings of anger, rage, depression, fear, abandonment, worthlessness, anxiousness and feeling trapped. Common methods of self-injury are cutting, picking scabs or wounds, scratching, burning self, self-hitting and head banging. Self-harmers do not want to commit suicide; self-abuse is an outward expression of deep, hidden and often-secret pain. They want intervention and love.

Respond to the child with out judgment; document the self-harm and contact help.

THE CHILD OF THE NARCISSIST

THE NPD IMAGINES IN THEIR HEAD THAT THEIR

BROOD SHOULD BE AROUND THEM AT ALL TIMES,

BECAUSE YOU ARE INCAPABLE OF LIVING YOUR LIFE

WITHOUT THEM. THIS IS THE BIRD THAT DOES

NOT

KICK THE CHICKS OUT OF THE NEST BECAUSE IT

DOES

NOT WANT THEM TO FLY.

THUS, IF THE CHILD OF THE NPD IS CAPABLE OF

GETTING AWAY AND GROWING UP ONCE AND FOR

ALL,

THEY ARE THE ENEMY TO THIS PARENT. NO ONE IS

ALLOWED TO LEAVE THE NPD'S KINGDOM UNLESS

IT

IS TO DO THEIR BIDDING.

JEANNINE K. VEGH, M.A., I.M.F.T.

TRANSFORMATIVE PSYCHOTHERAPY. LLC

CHAPTER 4. When Family is a Cult & Using Religion and Spirituality to Control

"OF ALL BAD MEN, RELIGIOUS BAD MEN ARE THE WORST" –C.S. LEWIS

Religious abuse is abuse administered under the guise of religion, including harassment or humiliation, which may result in psychological trauma. Religious abuse may also include misuse of religion for selfish, secular, or ideological ends such as the abuse of a clerical position.

- Keith Wright, *Religious Abuse*, Wood

The United Nations agrees that children should be protected from all forms of abuse, even that which could be hidden under the guise of religious teachings and activities. "

"Article 14 of the U.N. convention on the Rights if the Child guarantees that a child has the freedom to choose their own religion or spiritual beliefs and path. In article 5 of the same convention in Child Rights it signifies that the parents community or extended family does have the right and duty to provide in a matter consistent with ***evolving capacities*** of the child, while giving appropriate direction and guidance for that child to exercise their convention rights."

The mind and soul are often the last safe place for the abused to retreat and keep as their own place of sanctity, so when **abuse** administered under the guise of **religion**, including harassment or humiliation, it may result in psychological trauma.

Religious abuse may also include misuse of **religion** for selfish, secular, or ideological ends such as the **abuse** of a clerical position."

Religion can offer community and profound meaning, it can give a child the basis for living in an ethical and productive way, if it is not used as a tool to control or manipulate. Once fear is introduced then religion has ceased to be an outline for better living, fear is not the heart of any love principled god.

There is the cult of the church and similarly the cult of the family. The two are very comparable and share the same characteristics and the following lists can be used to check for both types of authoritarian cultish abuse. The cult of the family is much like the cult of the church except the cult of the family is lead by an authoritarian parent/guardian that demands extreme loyalty and inclusion to remain in the family or loved by the family. Often this parent will also use some form of twisted religious doctrine to back up their claims of "ownership" over the members, thoughts, feelings, and actions.

This chapter speaks volumes to me as someone who has witnessed first hand the damage that a willing narcissist can inflict by controlling a young mind through fear with religion. At this point you are now faced with a child who has been critically damaged emotionally from abuse and needs total reprogramming from spiritual abuse. In the end even if the child comes out moderately unscathed emotionally, "God", "Mercy" or "Love" may seem wildly incompatible. Spiritual journey are personal journeys we should not force anyone of any age to try and experience exactly as we have- because that is an impossible task- and only produces and inauthentic spiritual experience that serves to cheapen what could be a beautiful and deep moment for a person.

Churches have historically been safe spaces for individuals to connect with other and profess and practice worship of a divine entity. Millions of people successfully attend worship services and return to the outside world better for it, more thoughtful, peaceful and full of well-being. Often increasing overall satisfaction and reaching out to others who are in need by practicing love and peace-based ideologies. Religion is used often, to successfully cope with everyday stresses. In general being "religious" is seen as reaching a certain level of trustworthiness, something to aspire to, to draw close to and to admire. This makes it a perfect lambs clothing for a hungry wolf. Beware this type of emotional abuser, they are extremely destructive to the child, because they do not only ruin the sanctity of the home and the mind of the child, the abuser also pollutes any chance that the child may find escape of peace in spirituality.

CHECKLIST FOR ABUSIVE

RELIGIOUS PRACTICE

☐ When the religious practice begins to assert that:

☐ They are the only way to obtain happiness or be let into an afterlife "Heaven"

☐ Members must pledge their total allegiance and depend on the church doctrine to guide them in all aspects of their lives

☐ Suppresses Criticism, does not allow for questioning of doctrine or participation in branching out of thoughts concerning dogma

☐ Spout certain entitlements that only members can obtain spiritually.

☐ Authoritarian teaching, and over-emphasis on authority.

☐ Image Conscious, real believers are validated in their appearance, this alone signals their specialness to "God."

☐ Perfectionist, performance and conformity are rewarded while non-compliance is punished.

They have gone beyond simple guidance of a person or that person's "soul" towards enlightenment and charged right into "control." These places of worship are usually led by highly skilled narcissists and anti-social (in that their only gain is to recruit you to feed their hungry ego) emotional abusers. There is not one religion that has this trait; all religious activities are prone to drawing power hungry abusers to clamor for places of leadership. To a starving Narcissist being given the position of "gatekeeper" to the divine, these institutions look like an all you can eat buffet, with an unlimited source of supplies to hook up to.

Now we know that religions often attract stronger narcissistic types to feed, we can explore how emotionally abusive parents use this perfectly set up system to create an even tighter safety net for them.

In an article published by Rev. Rafael Martinez, who runs a group called Spiritwatch Ministries, the spiritual leader warns against spiritual abuse and likens the use of it to the building of a spiritual prison around those who are targeted. Rev. Martinz outlines the reflags that people should be wary of when considering if a person or group is using spiritual abuse to control them. HE calls these principles: I explain in further personal detail in italics.

SEVEN BARS OF RELIGIOUSLY ABUSIVE PRISONS

Absolute obedience to the elite - submission to all dictates of leaders at any price. *In the case of a child the elite would consist of the person in charge of their "wellbeing." While we naturally expect and want a child to show loving obedience to a parent or an adult in charge, this specific type of obedience is authoritarian and unquestionable in nature, leaving the child no room to create boundaries or insert their needs or wishes into their daily life.*

Extreme group conformity - undue compulsion to adopting a community code of conduct- *Controlling* *aspects such as friendships due to religious differences, denying age appropriate outings due to "religious differences", imprinting that other religions are scary, bad or evil and those people should be avoided. Being "forced" to dress, act, think, talk like the parent or religious community and to endure great shame, rejection, physical or emotion abuse of not followed to the letter.*

Suspension of critical thinking - group rejection of independent thought as sinful, demonic. *Telling a child if they do not follow through with a specific request they will go to Hell or they will be demonically attacked.*

Twisting of Scripture - misinterpretation of Biblical passages/teachings to magnify authority. *Cherry picking is often used, or twisting of meaning to make a point. If scripture is used to harm another, it is not a product of a loving God. "Spare the rod and Spoil the child" is NOT an invitation to beat a child for not being perfect.*

Phobic manipulation - using fear of punishment to intentionally control and dominate another. *"If you tell anyone we won't love you." "If you tell anyone, they will take you away." "If you don't do as I say you will go to Hell or (Insert deity here) won't love you anymore." Another example is of a church or a parent controlling a child's private actions such as telling them they will go to hell or that God is angry with* *them if they "touch themselves." This is a normal activity and while it should be done in **private** it should NEVER be controlled by anyone else, a parent, a church - anyone unless it becomes a fixation at which point it should be handles with respect for the child's feelings and privacy and forwarded to a professional who can help.*

Coerced confession of faults - forced pressure on the self and others to confess to "sins"

Abusive excommunication - brutal expulsion of members and harsh treatment afterwards. *If the child expresses a mind of needs of their own that do not comply with the wants of the parent or church, they are thrown out. A child is not an adult and therefore cannot be "thrown out." Locking the door on a frustrated, fearful or angry child is abuse, home is a place where they learn what is normal and throwing another person out a home and locking the door is NOT normal behavior. Another tactic that is used is to cut off contact, to simply "shun" or ignore the child, to turn away from them when they enter a room and to not respond to them verbally when they verbalize needs. Call social services immediately if a child alerts you to being expelled from their home or is in a situation where the community will not communicate with them.*

Red Flags for

Spiritual/Religious Abuse

Source: CSA resources about psychological manipulation, cultic groups, sects, and new religious movements. Cult checklist

☐ The child displays excessively zealous and unquestioning commitment to his/her caregiver in regards his/her belief system, and practices their caregivers belief system as LAW.

☐ Questioning, doubt, and dissent are discouraged or even punished.

☐ The parent dictates in great detail how the child should think, act, dress and feel based on their interpretation of the religion. This also includes whom they are allowed to associate with, what they are allowed to view, listen to or read. Where they should live if they are in a situation where parents are separated.

☐ The parent preaches elitism concepts, and states that they hold the only key to spiritual reward or safety.

- ☐ The parent/ Guardian is not accountable to any authorities such as teachers, police, other people of that faith or other authority figures on the child's life.

- ☐ The parent instills an us-verses—them mentality, which may causes conflict with wider society.

Religion in and of it's self is not a bad thing, it gives positive direction, hope and fellowship to millions people everyday but it can be a powerful tool to control young and innocent people. The effects are often catastrophic for the person who finally deprograms and breaks free. Every human being deserves the right to maintain an autonomous identity in which they cultivate their own ideas and beliefs; even children should be afforded the freedom to formulate their OWN identity separate from any caregiver, parent or guardian.

"ONE BELIEVES THINGS BECAUSE
ONE HAS BEEN CONDITIONED TO
BELIEVE THEM."
— ALDOUS HUXLEY, BRAVE NEW
WORLD

CHAPTER 5. The Helicopter Parenting Phenomenon

hel·i·cop·ter par·ent

Noun noun: helicopter parent, plural noun: helicopter parents

1. A parent who takes an overprotective or excessive interest in the life of their child or children. "Some college officials see all this as the behavior of an overindulged generation, raised by helicopter parents and lacking in resilience"

Word Origin 1980s: from the notion of the parent 'hovering like a helicopter' over the child or children.

Derivatives

1. Helicopter parenting n. (Oxford Dictionaries)

This is a touchy term for many people, who will see this term as a personal attack on their "motherly" instinct to protect a child they feel is at risk just by being alive in the world today. You look at the news, you read the paper, you take a quick dive into social media and there are a thousand examples of how dangerous the world is for a child to grow up in. Child molesters, killer clowns, bullies, mean teachers, poisoned candy, terrorist attacks, mass shootings, and super germs. law suits etc. etc.... So it would seem to many people that the person who is not completely overinvolved in their children's life providing up to the minute security is the abusive parent and not the other way around.

For the most part these "helicopter parents" are not aware that the level of obsessive control they exert is not helping save their child but actually causing developmental and social delays that will impede success and personal growth for decades after they leave home. Though it is not usually done out of spite or negligence, chronic and intense over-involvement does border and at times cross over into the realm of mental and emotional child abuse. The fallout from several decade of this type of over indulgent parenting has led to a counter movement called "Free-Range Parenting" a term coined my Lenore Skenazy, a woman made famous for letting her young child ride the subway home in a huge city with only a map and quarters to call home if they got lost. The child did make it home and she reports with a huge sense of self-accomplishment and pride. This isn't a book where I insert my personal feelings or promotions towards either style of parenting, because both styles attract certain kinds of abusers, the overinvolved and the nonexistent parent. Picking a style does not remove the parent from finding balance that is healthy for their particular child's personal needs. Each child is different but balance is key for raising a healthy child into a healthy adult. Healthy people will know there are age appropriate boundaries and also teachable moments when a child does have the capacity to excel in developing their budding independence.

Before I layout the red flag list to scan, I want to take a moment to present actual data and statistical findings that back up the notion that "helicopter parenting" is a dangerous practice for the child involved.

1ST – REALLY HOW DANGEROUS IS THE WORLD TODAY COMPARED TO OTHER TIMES IN HISTORY?

Christopher Ingraham of the Washington post did a piece on the reality of safety concerning kids in America. He reports that Child Mortality has steadily dropped since 1935, due to medical advances, networking to prevent child related crimes and a surge in improvements in technology.

In 1935 there were 450 deaths out of every 100,000 children ages 1-4. Today that number is less than 30 out 100,000!

The murder rate of children of all ages has dropped significantly since 1990's in 2008 the Bureau of

Justice released statistics stating that the homicide rate for children under the age of 14 was a record low of 1.5 cases per 100,00 kids ages 14-17 dove from 12 homicides per 100,000 in 1993 to 5.1 in 2008.

For children between the ages of 5 and 14, the chances of dying by any means are less than 1 in 10,000! That is about 0.01 %.

For the majority of those reading this and also for myself, we grew up sometime between the 1960's and the 1990's, which statistically were far ore dangerous times to grow up in. Yet what summer wasn't punctuated by bike rides around the neighborhood, walks to friend's homes down the block, sleepovers in the tents in the back yard or summer camps away from home that lasted for weeks? In fact we would have found it weird and irritating if our parents had followed us around dictating what activity we should be doing, telling us to stay in and watch TV because we could get hurt playing tag football or refusing to let us sleepover at a friends because "child molesters are everywhere."

But what about abduction? What if my child goes out with a group of friends and never comes home? To any caregiver, guardian or parent, that is a really terrifying idea that seems to be within the realm of possibility – everyday we get an Amber alert flashing across one of our screens, so it must be incredibly common occurrence and therefore keeping constant tabs on our children is the responsible thing to do?

Since 1997 – reports of any kind of child abduction has fallen over 40%. At the same time the population of the US has been steadily growing by over 30%, the rate of missing children reported in the US is less than 40% because we are pulling from a pool of more children.

If your child IS the roughly .01% that is abducted or molested you often don't need to look much further than your circle of friends and family. DoSomething.org summarizes the reality of abductions and sexual abuse into major categories.

Family members, often embroiled in some form of custody disputes, carry out 4 out 5 child abductions.

While 1 Out of 3 girls and 1 out of 5 boys will experience some for of sexual abuse before they reach the age of 18

90% of the sexual predators will be someone the child knows (not a stranger.)

68% are family members.

So why don't our expectations of danger match up to the statics provided by government agencies? Media. Media influences everything we do, what we think, what we buy, what we want and what we believe and we are bombarded on a daily, minute by minute basis by fear. Turn off the TV, News, Social Media posts that are perpetuating fear and start living in the now, get to know your family, your friends, your neighbors and that is your best defense against a potential predator.

2ND - WHAT IS THE ACTUAL NEGATIVE IMPACT IF ANY OF "OVER INVOLVEMENT"

Many parents are willing to overreach themselves, excessively intervene and cater to their children who do not receive any type of benefit from this behavior. It is a type of control for the parent, it helps them feel that maybe if they just take care of everything and know everything and control everything- nothing could possibly go wrong. When people feel they can control everything, they also feel they can avoid pain but that is not how the real world works. Dr. Lisa Firestone PhD writes about this in her article featured on Psychology Today, children raised this way do not grow to find independence, they are often stunted heavily in the areas that help them process self care, responsibility and weighing consequences. Growing up is a process of weaning a child from the parent so that they can learn through experience, this transition in vital to growing into a healthy adult with fully functioning psychological wellbeing. Children that are over parented often find themselves full of frustration, anxiety about doing even small tasks such as working or keeping a home and they harbor a great deal of resentment against their parents who treated them as though they weren't smart enough to figure anything out.

Another author, Joyce Catlett co-authored a book entitles Compassionate Child Rearing, stresses that it is imperative that parents live their own lives wand participate in their own interests outside of their children's. Parents cannot function at 100%v if they are not happy or fulfilled and children are emotional sponges, soaking up the emotions of their loved ones. In the end the child will not understand why the parent seems to be unfulfilled, they will equate it to themselves and who they are and that is devastating.

A study conducted by BYU found that over parented children had a myriad of issues when approaching their tween and teen years, these children seemed less able to focus or engage in schoolwork, they also had a higher instance of participating in high risk behaviors such as unprotected, multiple partner "hook ups" (sex) and binge drinking and countered with low self esteem. A professor of Developmental Psychology at The University of Warwick Medical School in the UK lead a study in how helicopter parenting undermined positive parenting, he found that overprotective parents actually increase social stress by creating children who attract bullies, this information was gathered from over 70 studies on more than 200,000 children. Parents or guardians that attempt to protect their children from negative social interactions, create more issues than if they had allowed the child to learn from and navigate these situations themselves. Major areas that are impacted for these over parented children are important to healthy growth and development in a social world. These include an:

An inability to problem solve even simple issues or participate in successful conflict resolution or negotiating for a win-win situation.

Children have lower emotional intelligence, this allows a person to be self-aware, to effectively manage their own emotions and to be aware of others socially, knowing how to manage relationships.

All of these skills allow children to be healthier and more resilient throughout their lives.

Over parented children can have unrealistic expectations, this leads to immense frustration and depression later in life when they don't achieve what they expected to. It is good to teach a child that life is not always fair, it is not always easy and sometimes several attempts may be required to achieve a goal or redirection is key to finding an alternative path to success. These children often see the beginning of the prospect and the end- they see what others have achieved but do not understand the journey between the two points is vital to achieving what they want. Kids pitter out halfway through trying something new, or stop immediately when confronted with opposition, negative feedback or failure. This is a set up for disappointment and anxiety.

Kids that never have to deal with the consequences of not adhering to rules grow up into adults that do not understand what it is to be a reliable, dependable tem player. By the time a child is ten, they have the emotional IQ to take responsibility for mistakes, if they forget to do their homework, they need to talk to their teacher. If they lie or steal, they need to apologies and ask what they can do to mend the harm, these are extremely important social skills, and immature, selfish anti-social behavior is rarely tolerated in the adult world, leaving these children art risk for self-isolation and social failure.

Abusive Over parenting

Checklist

☐ The child needs to consult their parents before making an age appropriate decision about ANYTHING.

☐ The parent intervenes with other authority figures to take the brunt of any consequences the child may have incurred. They may even blame the authority figure and say it is their fault that they just don't understand the child well enough to say negative things about them.

☐ The child is drowning with extra curricular activities; they have so many activities, activities they may not even enjoy, and so may that they can't even take a minute for themselves.

☐ An adult, preferably the parent, supervises all extra curricular activities.

☐ The child is given excessive praise at inappropriate times to avoid letting the child feel negative emotions. Even if the child does nothing noteworthy the parent tells them how wonderful they are- while praise is a wonderful tool, unwarranted praise breeds narcissism later in life.

☐ Not allowing children to engage in certain forms of play. Not allowing them to work their way out of certain situations with other children, or intervening to avoid any conflict.

☐ The parent does the child's homework for them to avoid mistakes or failure to meet due dates.

☐ The parent expresses germ phobic tendencies and compounds this by not allowing the child to participate in safe play because of the obsession.

☐ The parent is keeping constant tabs on a child at all times, not allowing them out of their sight, placing tracking devices on their phones or texting/calling constantly to "check up."

Like any other behavior that may seem emotionally destructive for the child involved, it is important to involve the appropriate authorities to intervene and not attempt to do this, the helicopter parent most likely won't see their behavior as abusive and with close off the conversation as fast as possible. This might need the help of a team or a psychologist to address the behaviors and really open the person up to realizing that they are hindering their child's emotional, psychological and social progress.

"THE GREATER A CHILD'S TERROR,
AND THE EARLIER IT IS
EXPERIENCED, THE HARDER IT
BECOMES TO DEVELOP A STRONG
AND HEALTHY SENSE OF SELF."
— NATHANIEL BRANDEN, SIX
PILLARS OF SELF-ESTEEM

Chapter 6. Codependency & Enmeshment

co·de·pend·en·cy

/ˌkōdəˈpendənsē/

Noun

Excessive emotional or psychological reliance on a partner, typically a partner who requires support due to an illness or addiction.

Oxford Dictionary

Enmeshment: is a state of cross-generational bonding within a family, whereby a child (normally of the opposite sex) becomes a surrogate spouse for their mother or father. The term is also applied more generally to engulfing codependent relationships where an unhealthy symbiosis is in existence.

R. Abell, *Own Your Own Life* (1977) p. 119-22

Parental enmeshment is very much like the roots of two entangled plants, on the surface they seem to be independent of one another but if you tug one the other feels the pain and discomfort. In the same way a parent overlays their own emotions and issues on a child usually starting at a young age, until the child has no idea where their feelings begin or the parent's end. They are not allowed to feel their own joys, fears or needs, they must constantly make sure not to tug or pull too much or the entangled roots between the caregiver and the child will cause both great pain. An enmeshed family is a family where members are so closely involved in one another's lives that they limit the healthy function of each individual's ability to be independent. This is closely related to Co-Dependency, which often goes hand in hand with Enmeshment. Co-dependency is a learned behavior that is passed from one generation to the other. It is a type of relationship addiction in which a parent (or anyone in a relationship) maintains a one-sided, emotionally destructive and abusive bond. Often the co-dependent parent is trying to act as a buffer between their child and another harmful caregiver, usually a narcissist. The emotional drain that the co-dependent experiences as maintaining a willing "supply" for the narcissist as well as providing left over emotional resources just for maintaining some kind of balance leaves little for the child.

A Narcissist is basically a huge power drain, they hook onto their victim and extract emotional energy relentlessly until the person is a shell, then they love bomb them until they seems to be full enough to feed off of again. A Co-dependent parent is providing a steady supply for the narcissistic parent/partner/guardian and doing so willingly but in doing so not leaving enough emotional energy to raise a healthy child. In many cases the **co-dependent** will ask the child to step in and fulfill an inappropriate role such as partner, they will use **enmeshment** as a tool to bind the child emotionally and make them less resistant to pulling away. Any type of emotional independence is felt as severe emotional pain to the co-dependent and enmeshment creates a situation where the child does not have their own feelings autonomous from the parent so they feel extreme fear and pain as well.

HOW DOES CO-DEPENDENCY/ENMESHMENT BEHAVIOR HARM A CHILD?

Source: AllaboutCoucniling.com

The co-dependent has no emotional resources available for a child. Co-Dependency is a compulsive drive to satisfy the needs of a very selfish and un-satisfy able person. Co-dependents will use coercion, threats, manipulation in order to attempt controlling the narcissist, to no avail, Narcissist are beyond control, they truly care nothing about the other people they encounter and see them as an emotional food source. The Narcissist needs other peoples heightened emotions to feel anything at all. Ross A. Rosenberg, writer for the publication "The Blog" explains that this is just a series of useless hamster wheel style experiences that weaken the co-dependent further. "Tired and beaten down, they often shut down and disconnect from their parental responsibility to protect their children (and themselves)."

Codependent people have a greater tendency than others to get involved in unhealthy or "toxic relationships. Codependent people have a weak sense of what a healthy boundary looks like. Children of co-dependents may be exposed to an endless cycle of emotionally unreliable, unsteady, dangerous romantic partners as the co-dependent parent attempts to cling to any relationship that will last. No matter what negative things occur within the relationship, even at the expense of their child (sexual, physical, verbal, emotional abuse, drug and alcohol addiction) the co-dependent parent will make excuses for the narcissistic person and they will be negligent in reacting in appropriate ways to create a safe living environment for their children.

Co-dependency creates mental health issues in children. With the rise of over anxious parenting and co-dependent behaviors since the 1980's it isn't surprising that Anxiety disorders in children are also on the rise. According to Raychelle Cassada Lohmann MS, in Licensed Practical Nursing 13% of children are now experiencing separation and social anxiety and that is a disturbingly high number of children, she believes that it directly correlates to over parenting and co-dependency issues in parents.

Co-Dependent parents participate in strange thinking and tell their children things that do not foster a sense of self-reliance, positive coping skills or emotional management. They may imply that the child

Should not discuss their feelings, or get upset or distant if emotions are involved in a conversation.

Should not discuss problems, fears, concerns or needs.

Suggest that the child just get over it, move one, suck it up and not be a crybaby.

Never give praise even when perfection is being sought, continually tell the child to work harder or be better.

Expect the child to strive to meet unrealistic expectations- tell them they are not allowed to come home unless they get a 4.0 in all of their classes.

Use the motto "Do as I say, not as I do" to relieve themselves of the responsibility to fix their own issues before making demands o their child to fix theirs.

CODEPENDENCY CREATES AN ONSLAUGHT OF MINI ISSUES LATER IN LIFE THAT BEGIN TO ADD UP INTO AN AVALANCHE OF SELF-HARMING BEHAVIORS.

☐ Low self esteem, the need to be in control, excessive need to please others.

☐ Anxiety and Stress, extreme worry, not feeling good enough.

☐ Non-assertive communication, blames self for other peoples problems, inability to trust.

☐ Willing to take any friend or partner no matter the emotional cost because they are afraid of being alone.

☐ Intimacy problems, difficulty making decisions, chronic anger and outbursts.

How Enmeshment affects a Child

Enmeshment isn't necessarily exclusively it's own category of abuse, it can be a trait that is carried by a skilled narcissist as well. "Narcissist Child", an extremely informative and deep well of information for those dealing with Narcissism outlines enmeshment and the fallout that precedes it.

The researcher explains that a narcissist uses enmeshment as a tool to reverse the roles of the child and the parent, the child is then expected to provide a continual supply of emotional gratification and meet that parents needs. The Narcissist does not provide the child with any type of guidance, the child is left to stumble blindly through their most important developmental years – grade school, preteen and puberty unprotected from any threat that may come along. The child suffers a great deficiency in affection and nurturing, they have a hard time seeing themselves as a person separate from the parent that they must take care of. This is because they are fused together like the tree that grew around the bicycle over several decades- what were once two separate beings has now grown together into one.

Enmeshment Co-Dependency Immediate Issues:

The Parent will use guilt as their greatest weapon: As a child grows older the parent will heap as much guilt on them as they feel is necessary to get the child to meet their unrelenting need, soon the child will begin to experience guilt as a central emotional response in their life and if they feel that they are not meeting other peoples needs they will feel crushed by the guilt that accompanies this perceived failure.

The child will choose one of two routes to deal with the unhealthy behaviors.

The child will not develop mentally or emotionally and remained stunted, this child will continue on into children remaining dependent on their parents, the narcissist will get to keep their "mini me" and the child will continue to provide a lifetime supply of emotional energy for the parent to syphon as the adult child slowly sinks deeper and deeper into depression and suffering.

The child will become repulsed by the enmeshment and pull away. As they reach the teen years they will seek unsafe methods of obtaining independence, in some cases that might be jumping into relationships and trying to form quick bonds in order to leave the situation, or it make take the form of running away and choosing life on the street over the emotional abuse suffered at home. Even if the child remains in the home the emotional void left from the abuse leads them to attempt to fill it with risky behaviors and different forms of addiction. Once the child begins to need support they are often pulled back into the unhealthy relationship and the enmeshment begins again.

LONG-TERM EFFECTS OF ENMESHMENT

The result is an adult that does not function emotionally at the level they could, exhibiting destructive behaviors:

☐ They have no healthy sense of identity, they are always partly their "parent"

☐ Limited ability to self soothe during times of turmoil, the adult victim will look for others to calm the feelings and provide emotional stability.

☐ Feel the need to get approval for ever detail in their lives, asking people who aren't emotionally ʼse or appropriate to give them feedback about ʼal issues.

☐ Have weak or non-existent boundaries, an inability to say no when others demand too much time or energy.

☐ Constantly will feel guilty if they do not run to their parents side and fulfill every last request, cannot say no, feels it would be disrespectful or would bring out negative reactions that they would rather avoid.

☐ Discards individual dreams or pursuits that would make them a better version of them to care for the parent's wishes and demands.

☐ Practices "conditional love." Which will lead to a cycle of disappointing and unfulfilling relationships. This love is a learned aspect, learned from the parent who only gives conditional love.

☐ Will experience extreme amounts of fear, fear about how to proceed with the future, fear of failure that leaves a person stuck in a discouraging lifestyle, fear of trying new things, fear of being rejected. This hinders the adult child from really experiencing their potential.

☐   Fear that the world is a dangerous place and that autonomy will lead to harm, the narcissist will tell her child that the world is scary and the child cannot survive with out her.

CHECK LIST FOR THE ENMESHED

CHILD

☐ Child seems to be closer to one parent than the other.

☐ Child is the source of emotional support for the caregiving adult.

☐ Child is "Best Friends" with the parent, instead of having peers as friends.

☐ Parent over shares personal information with the child.

☐ Parent is over involved in personal activities or developing the child's "talents."

☐ Parent takes credit for or expresses excessive pride in the child's achievements.

☐ One parent gives the child "special" gifts and privileges.

☐ Child has been told that they are the "favorite, most lovable or most talented" child.

☐ The parent prefers the company of the child to that of their romantic partner.

☐ The child feels guilty when they spend time away from one of the parents.

☐ The child feels unable to make friends or do things outside of the home because it would hurt the parent.

☐ The child idolizes the parent with no regard for any shortcomings.

☐ None of the child's potential friends are "good enough"

☐ The child's parents are inappropriately aware of the child's sexuality.

☐ Parent has made inappropriate sexual remarks or violated privacy.

CHECKLIST FOR PARENTAL

NEGLECT OR ABUSE

☐ The child's needs seem to be ignored or neglected.

☐ There is a great deal of conflict between the child and one parent

☐ The child is called hurtful names by the parent

☐ One parent sets ridiculously high standards for the child.

☐ Parent is extremely critical of the child.

☐ The child has felt like hiding, or has fantasies of running away.

☐ The child's family seems more emotionally intense than other families.

The child shows relief when they are able to leave home.

☐ The child feels invaded by the parent.

☐ The child "owns" their parent's unhappiness.

CHECKLIST FOR THE CHILD OF

THE CO-DEPENDENT

☐ Child has difficulty saying no, even if they know they shouldn't do it.

☐ The child feels responsible for the problems of others, even when they did not cause the problem.

☐ The child does not take time to be good to them because they feel it is selfish.

☐ The child needs outside approval so that they can accept themselves.

☐ The child cannot even handle constructive criticism because it makes them feel like a total failure.

☐ The child is timid and avoidant when they feel they may make a scene that will upset the parent or other people.

☐ Once the child receives approval for something they become obsessive about doing that same thing in order to find more approval.

☐ The child will seek perfection and become angry and impatient if they cannot obtain it easily.

☐ The child becomes easily defensive in order to protect what positive self-image they do have imperfections are seen as devastating.

☐ The child will feel panicky if they are not in control of the situation

☐ ▨▨▨ ▨▨▨▨▨▨▨▨▨▨▨e▨▨▨▨▨▨▨▨▨▨i▨▨▨▨▨▨▨▨▨▨▨▨

☐ The child has very low self-esteem, they may try to hide it but they don't really like themselves.

☐ The child blames and criticizes others for their circumstances and negative feelings.

☐ The child makes friends with unhealthy people, troublemakers, and low achievers.

☐ The child seldom asks for help for fear of bothering someone.

☐ The child chooses to do things themselves rather than risk being disappointed by others not achieving their lofty expectations.

☐ The child reacts negatively to trying new things; they do not transition well between activities.

An Ending Note

As we wrap up this little book of red flags and explanations it is important to emphasize that if you have concerns the proper authority should be contacted. There are disorders and spectrums that mimic some of the signs through out the past five chapters and it is important to let a professional decide what the root of any behavioral problem is. This book is also not intended as a tool for "witch hunting" against parents that you don't agree with or like, if this is just a strategy to harm another parent a judge or a councilor will see past it very quickly. It is not suggested that these signs be used to manipulate or purposefully harm another person. If you are reading this because you feel concerned that you know a child that may be experiencing emotional abuse in one form or another read a little further to see what steps you need to take to provide advocacy for them. I hope that you have found this manual to be interesting and informative, it is my first adventure into the world of self-publishing and I would be very thankful to receive your comments and ratings so that I can continue to improve my writing and researching for the publics use.

Advice from Healthline.com on handling abuse wither from another person or recognizing the tendency coming from yourself

WHO SHOULD I TELL?

"If you or someone you know is being emotionally abused, contact your local children or family services departments. Ask to speak to a counselor. You can also call the National Child Abuse Hotline at 1-800-4ACHILD (1-800-422-4453) for information on free help in your area. Many family services departments allow callers to report suspected abuse anonymously.

If it's not possible to contact a family services agency, ask someone you trust, such as a teacher, relative, doctor, or clergyperson for help. You might be able to help a family you are concerned about by offering to babysit or run errands. However, don't put yourself at risk or do anything that would increase risk for the child you're concerned about.

Some forms of abuse, such as yelling, may not be immediately dangerous. However, other forms, such as allowing children to use drugs, can be instantly harmful. If you have any reason to believe you or a child you know is in danger, call 911 immediately.

No one deserves to be abused. If you're worried about what will happen to the child's parents or

Caregivers, remember that getting them help is the best way to show them you love them.

"SPEAK THE TRUTH

EVEN IF YOUR VOICE SHAKES"

What Can I Do If I Think I May Be Harming My Child in This Way?

"Even the best parents have yelled at their children or used angry words in times of stress. That's not necessarily abusive. However, you should consider calling a counselor if you notice a pattern in your behavior. Parenting is the toughest and the most important job you will ever do. Seek the resources to do it well. For example, change your behavior if you regularly use alcohol or illegal drugs. These habits can affect how well you care for your children."

Sources for More... Important Terms

In attempting to make a guidebook that deals primarily with listing red flag behaviors in a little over 100 pages I could not possibly fit all issues associated to emotional abuse. I suggest visiting the exceptionally informational website **http://flyingmonkeysdenied.com** to see their detailed glossary of abuse terminology for further identification of possible abuse techniques and results of abuse. Another wonderful resource is **http://narcissismschild.com**. I have absolutely no affiliation with these sites but found them to be two of the most comprehensive resources on the subject of emotional abuse and recommend checking them out if you have the chance.

ONE LAST THING...

If you enjoyed this book or found it useful I'd be very grateful if you'd post a short review on Amazon. Your support really does make a difference and I read all the reviews personally so I can get your feedback and make this book even better.

NOTES & DOCUMENTATION

Use the space provided in the back of the book to use for documenting behaviors.

Notes & Documentation

Notes & Documentation

Notes & Documentation

Notes & Documentation

Notes & Documentation

23268719R00073

Printed in Poland
by Amazon Fulfillment
Poland Sp. z o.o., Wrocław